Shards

Shards

Mashiko Poetry
by Ann Holmes

Ann Holmes

Turn of River Press

Cover photograph by Ann Holmes; vase by Takeshi Shiraishi

Library of Congress Card Catalog Number
2003-111036

ISBN 0-938999-16-8

Turn of River Press
6 Rushmore Circle
Stamford, CT 06905–1029
203–322–5438

Acknowledgments

Excerpt from THE CAVE, copyright © José Saramago e Editorial Caminho, SA, Lisboa-2000, English translation copyright © 2002 by Margaret Jull Costa, reprinted by permission of Harcourt, Inc.

Excerpt compiled from two translations of *TAO TE CHING* by Stephen Mitchell, Harper & Rowe, 1988, and *Tao Ching* by John C.H. Wu, Shambhala Classics, 1961.

Excerpt from *The Windows of Life*, a monograph on Kawai Kanjiro by E. Ushita, printed by the Tanshiki Printing Co., Kyoto Japan.

Grateful acknowledgments to the editors of the following journals in which some of the poems in this collection appeared: "Rice Paddies," *Red Wheelbarrow*; "Threat of Immortality," *The Connecticut River Review*; and "Unchanging" and "Bricks," *The Asian Pacific American Journal*.

To my mentor, Joan Larkin, for the heart and spirit of her insightful critiques.

To Billy Collins, Jane Flanders, Suzanne Gardinier, Thomas Lux, Anneliese Wagner, and Jean Valentine for encouragement and guidance.

To Yukako Hayakawa, for her help conducting interviews of Mashiko potters, and along with her husband, Yoshinori, for their hospitality to me when I returned to study pottery in Mashiko.

To Hiroshi and Yumiko Kawajiri, and their children, Natsumi, Emi and Teku, for the opportunity to experience from the inside the nerve and rhythm of the potters' life.

To all the Mashiko potters, especially the former Mashiko potter, Gerd Knapper, who introduced me to potters, historians, and people involved with the Mashiko pottery industry; the Nakayamas, proprietors of the Nakayama Mingeiten, who directed me to potters by foot-paths, across rice paddies; for the friendship and support of Harvey Young; Naobumi Kubota; Sui Nagakura; Hiroshi Seto and Hiroya Hirosaki; and to members of the English Clubs at Waseda and Keio Universities who did translations and conducted many interviews.

To members of my writing group, Lou Barrett, Alene Bricken, and Elsa Nad for intelligent listening and feedback, and additionally, to Peggy Heinrich and Jacqueline Steiner for their significant editorial assistance.

To Jack, Kip, and Megan Holmes, Lia Minonne, Dale Shaw, David Connor, Zdena Heller, and Sylvia Clark for their belief in me and my commitment to Mashiko.

To my publishers, Ralph and Linda Nazareth, for transforming my poems and photographs into an integrated whole.

To my friends and family who have encouraged my effort to make Mashiko live on these pages.

...a shard of pottery on the ground is not only what it is at present it is also what it was in the past when it was something else, as well as what it might become in the future....
José Saramago

Introduction

Mashiko is a folk-pottery town located a hundred miles northwest of Tokyo. When one hears "Mashiko," the initial reaction is to identify it as the home of Shoji Hamada, Mashiko's former "Master Potter" and "National Cultural Treasure." It is also home to several hundred artist-potters, some of whom you will encounter in "Shards." A popular tourist site, the town attracts the discriminating pottery lover as well as the casual browser seeking affordable tableware rendered in earthtone glazes and swish-of-the-brush motifs.

I lived in Tokyo in the early 1970s and visited several of the Japanese major kilnsites. These date back to the medieval era, when the Tea Masters, sensing the rustic beauty of common storage jars and rice bowls made by artisans, appropriated them into the aesthetics of the tea ceremony. Today, descendants from the name-kilnsites continue to reproduce the glazes and forms sanctioned by those Tea Masters hundreds of years ago.

Unlike these famous kilnsites, Mashiko attracted men and women after World War II who were new to the field: sociologists, philosophers, teachers, historians, businessmen, noodle-makers, musicians, and painters. Not subject to the constraints imposed by tradition, the Mashiko artist-potters were free to try out different techniques and glazes and develop distinct and innovative styles.

A visit to Mashiko left me wondering what drew people from such varied backgrounds to pottery and to this town. One day, while photographing Hamada at the opening of his kiln, I asked why no one had written a book on Mashiko artist-potters. "Too much is written about me," he replied, deflecting the question back to himself. "It's time I turn Mashiko over to the potters." His remarks implanted the idea that I might be the one to write such a book.

With assistance from the English clubs at Keio and Waseda Universities, I began to interview Mashiko potters. On her first day in Mashiko, Yukako Horyuchi, an English language student who lived with our family in Tokyo and became my principal interpreter, exclaimed, "I didn't know such people existed outside of novels!"

I returned to Connecticut and attended New York University, where I wrote my doctoral thesis on "The Transition of the Artisan-Potter to the Artist-Potter in Mashiko." After a while, writing about pottery wasn't enough for me. I wanted to experience making it myself. I returned to Mashiko and apprenticed with Hiroshi Kawajiri, and lived with his family.

This book grew out of a year of independent study with Joan Larkin in the Masters degree program in poetry at Sarah Lawrence College.

"Shards" is divided into two sections. Part One, "Clay," is a poetry-pottery memoir, a narrative of my perceptions and misconceptions as a fifty-year-old American woman apprentice. Part Two, "Potters," consists of poems based on interviews with artist-potters. I had been curious to learn if the idealized life of the potter would hold up under the rigorous routine of the firing cycle. Few, however, addressed this issue, preferring to focus on aesthetics. Writing from the artist-potters' perspective, I have tried to preserve the individual character that animated each voice. These poems are my response to an image, a phrase, a dialogue, exploring the metaphoric and mythic alchemy of clay and fire.

History of Mashiko Pottery

Pottery production in Mashiko dates back to the mid-nineteenth century. Keizaburo Otsuka is considered to have founded the first kiln there, making kitchenware for the local feudal lord, temples and farmers. By 1863, five kilns were in operation. Soon afterwards, Mashiko ware began to be exported to Tokyo. The Mashiko Pottery Institute opened in 1904, offering technical training in place of the traditional apprenticeship system.

In the early twentieth century, Japanese ceramic tableware production was significantly affected by a number of factors tied to industrialization and social migration to the cities. With the introduction of gas and coal for cooking in 1919, pottery could not withstand the intense heat and was replaced by metal pots and pans. In cities, moreover, where living space was at a premium, glass and metal fit more easily into kitchen cupboards. Newcomers, anxious to hide their provincial roots, preferred machine-made kitchenware to handmade pottery. The market for ceramic ware improved somewhat following the 1923 earthquake, which almost leveled Tokyo and Yokohama and created an immediate demand for new household goods.

Depressed production in Mashiko was offset, however, by the role that the town came to play in the developing *mingei* movement. Early in the twentieth century, a group of young painters, potters, and poets advocated the revival and preservation of traditional Japanese crafts. Soetsu Yanagi, Shoji Hamada, the British potter Bernard Leach, and Kenkichi Tomimoto traveled throughout Japan, urging craftsmen not to abandon their traditional skills, which were rapidly being made redundant by industrialization. They arranged craft exhibitions to educate the public. Yanagi invented the term *mingei* to celebrate the beauty of everyday objects made by unknown craftsmen. He enumerated three basic principles of the *mingei* ideal: anonymity, simplicity, and frugality. By its very ambiguity, "people's art" implied both the user and the maker.

Pottery was where the *mingei* movement was most completely realized. The potter, Shoji Hamada, applied the tenets of the *mingei* ideal to his life-style and work, thus establishing a model for the potters who succeeded him. Hamada had studied pottery at the Tokyo and Kyoto Technical Colleges before coming under the influence of the *mingei* movement. He accompanied Bernard Leach to St. Ives in Cornwall, England, where he lived for three years and supervised the building of Leach's kiln modeled after the traditional Japanese multi-chambered *noborigama*. When Hamada returned to Japan in 1924, he settled in Mashiko.

Natives like to tell the story of how Hamada's mother packed his school lunchbox each day with a small Mashiko *dobae* teapot, and that his love for this teapot brought him to the town. More likely it was the proximity of Mashiko to Tokyo, the good supply of clay, and Mashiko's reputation as a minor folkware kilnsite that drew him there. From this point on, the history of Mashiko is closely aligned with the biography of Hamada, who became the "Master Potter" of the town and was designated "a Living National Cultural Treasure" by the Japanese government in 1955. During his first year in Mashiko, Hamada held a one-man exhibition in Tokyo that was a sell-out. Suddenly Mashiko was known as "the home of Shoji Hamada."

The pottery Hamada made when he first came to Mashiko bore little if any resemblance to native tableware, yet it was compatible with the folkware genre. Gradually, Hamada began to adapt Mashiko designs and forms within his work. At the same time, he researched glazes and designs from the history of oriental ceramics, rediscovering techniques that he integrated into his contemporary folkware. His work was characterized by earth-tone glazes, simplified forms, heavy clay bodies, and abstract and organic decorative motifs. Hamada was known and admired throughout Japan, and following the Second World War, his life and pottery were publicized by the Japanese government. Paradoxically, fame and the high prices transformed his folkware into collector's items,

x

and compromised the *mingei* aesthetic and ideal of anonymity and frugality.

Attracted by Hamada's example, people came to study pottery in Mashiko after the Second World War. Most remained in the town and established themselves as independent potters. Some continued in the style of Hamada. Others distanced themselves from the original *mingei* movement and developed a personal style, characterized by experimental forms and unconventional firing and glazing techniques. These potters consciously identified themselves as "artist-potters." They maintained, nonetheless, a strong sense of craft, and a tie to nature and tradition. Alongside these artist-potters, family workshops continued to produce folk-style tableware.

Table of Contents

Clay

Potters

Table of Photographs

Clay

Potters

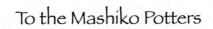

To the Mashiko Potters

We make a vessel from a lump of clay
but it is the emptiness within
that contains.

Tao Teh Ching
Lao Tzu

Clay

Return

I dreamt I'm here
so many times
but in my dreams
it never rains.

Shibaraku deshita...

that split-
second
when

the ache
of absence
is present.

How could I forget
opening an umbrella
in a circle of umbrellas?

Monorail to Tokyo

A woman in a black kimono
and her mini-skirted daughter smile

at the three umbrellas
puddling by our feet.

Across the aisle
a drunk slumps

on a flowered shoulder.
The shoulder moves away.

High school boys, backpacks
crammed with books, lunge

for empty seats. Shoved
by a classmate, one

bumps the drunk.
He bolts upright.

Head droops, body sways,
until he's boneless as before.

Black eyes scan black eyes.
He's a bad boy,

not the bum
he'd be back home.

Charm of Old Japan

The train's loudspeaker cheeps:
thank you for... please don't forget....

I watch the tracks until the train becomes a dot.
Yukako drives up, breathless.

I found a thatched-roof house you can rent
in a bamboo grove
across from a trout farm—
remote—
six miles from town.

We drive to a ramshackle hut.
Yukako reaches her hand through
tattered shoji and unlatches
the door. We kick off our sandals.
Mouse turds roll,
kicked by our bare toes.

I'll help you clean—

    Heat?
    none.

    Kitchen?
    zinc sink.

    Bath?
    trout pond?

My body cannot live here.

Kitchen Out of Focus

Yukako clattering pots and pans
a room away reminds me
of the time before words:
    what's that?
        what's it for?
            when I mistook
cigar and cigarette smoke for air,
before Granny shrieked:
I see your milk on the floor, and willed
my glass to spill, before
I remembered to forget
what I wasn't meant to see.

Mending

Do you smell garlic and ginger simmering?
Do you feel the prick of my needle?
Do you know the jacket I'm mending is cut from a kimono bought
    this morning at the second-hand shop?
Do you surmise my eyes won't converge on the eye
    of the needle?
Do you cover your ears when I yell Help to Yukako?
Do you catch Yukako coming out of the kitchen to rethread
    my needle?
Do you miss me biting off the thread?
Smell that garlic—makes you want to lick the air!

Right Wrong Road

Lost, Yukako swerves, skids
front wheels spin the air
    A potter runs over.
    Calls his neighbor.
The two confer.
We climb out. They realign the car.
    We're invited to tea.
    Yukako jabs a thumb at me.
She's looking for a place to work.
I'm unskilled....
    Yukako elbows me.
    In Japanese she means.
The potter is on the way to Chiba,
van jammed with pots.
    He lights a cigarette.
    She could work here.
His wife seems as surprised as I.
He drives off for cigarettes?
    Chiba?

Hiroshi Kawajiri

My Room

We climb upstairs
with no downstairs—

a de Chirico painting
suspended in air.

Beneath us is an open shed
stacked with firewood:

walls and ceilings and floors
of torn-down houses.

I breathe in the hemp-scent
of freshly laid *tatami* mats.

A rooster crows.
A dog barks.

Outside the picture-window, I see a red
sunset in a pure white sky—

a parody of The Land of the Rising Sun? the flag?

Yumiko opens a door to what I fear most:

a hole-in-the-ground, squat-down, indoor-outhouse.

Set-Up

A borrowed radio plays Bach Suites.
　　My clothes I've hung on nails
　　　　and stashed between pots.

My futon is patterned with fans and waves
　　and pink chrysanthemums
　　　　big as fists.

When I ask for a heater
　　Yumiko brings a winter kimono
　　　　lined in silk.

Children's Concert

Annsan, ofuro! Into the bath,
eldest to youngest, then me.
Chin-deep, I soak.

Natsumi, clad in brand new
white-white underpants,
invites me to a concert.

On the shiny black Yamaha
Emi practices with two hands
for her pre-school play.

Natsumi zips through
Emi's piece she
played two years ago.

With giant chopsticks
Tekyu clangs on a pan. More
than content, I'm happy.

Kawajiri Family
& Ann Holmes

Just for Show

Shifting West to East,
    the haziness of me
        in your dream
      caught me feeling
a prisoner.

I send you back a dream
    in which my hands
        are bound
      but the manacles
are just for show—

a ploy to appease
    the authorities.
        That my hands
      are bound hardly
matters. Yesterday

Sensei asked
    if at home
        I had a maid.
    I replied,
I *am* the maid.

Alarm Cock

3:45 A.M.
our rooster crows, echoed
by every rooster in the valley.

7:00 A.M.
The American Armed Forces Network broadcasts
English lesson for today:

The pen on the table is blue, isn't it?

No, it's black.

I snatch the black pen off the table and write:

3:45 A.M.
our rooster crows, echoed
by every rooster in the valley.

No Way to Start the Day

I air my futon, quilt and sheets
    on the window sill
    just as I see Yumiko do.
    Blue white and pink they fall.

I empty my dishpan
    when Sensei puts
    his bucket
    under the faucet.

The dirty water splashes
    his toe-socks—
    each toe
    gloved like a finger.

Fifty-Pound Sacks of Clay

The co-op truck grinds to a halt,
bed piled high with plastic sacks of clay.
Clay's here, Sensei shouts.

I run downstairs past
the hole-in-the-ground toilet
I never thought I'd get used to.

Yumiko (who weighs no more
than two sacks) lifts clay, lighter
than her eight-year-old daughter.

I tug at clay, gray
and sun-warmed—heavy
but not that heavy.

Preschool Workbook

Emi x's my mistakes:

the apple-cheeked

hiragana letters I ink

in spider-lines to

boy   girl   ball

flower   leaf   tree

sun   moon   stars.

English Lesson, Second Grade

Thunk goes Natsumi's schoolbag. *Tadaima!* I'm home!

Natsumi runs into the garden where we are drinking tea.
Swipes a strawberry off her mother's plate.

> *We learned English today.*
> YOU—she points at us.
> I—she taps her chest.
> YOU + I = WE.

Imagine, one word
  just one word
  for children
  and grown-ups
  together.

Pantomime

Bug-hot muggy, I wash glaze off boards.
In the field below Sensei plants potatoes.
Suddenly he's behind me. Loops a rope
around my waist.
He ties the other end to a drain-pipe.
I'm ballast!
He lowers the drain pipe down
                                    down
                                            down.
Staggers, his arms flapping birdwings.
He pretends he's me, falling down
                                    down
                                            down.

Perfection

My bowls that ought
to be the same aren't.

Sensei lights a cigarette.
Puffs a perfect smoke ring.

I watch it halo
his bald head.

He demotes me
to sake cups.

Reaching over the clay
spinning on my wheel

with finger and thumb
he pulls a perfect cup.

Ghost-Pots

strewn about the kiln, warn
what went wrong before
might go wrong again:

warped, cracked,
bald-spots, pots
puddled with glaze,

jugs won't pour,
a leaky vase, lids
glazed shut,

some looking as fit
as you and I, but
damaged within.

Ghost Pots

Foreigner

No name things spin
off my wheel.

I'm deaf
to your clay words.

You expect me to be odd—
shira-nai hito—a know-nothing person.

Do you know
what I don't know?

Dropping Dead in Mashiko

Early this morning a neighbor found
Atsuya Hamada dead
in his garden.

Yumiko said:

> *if Atsuya had a wife....*
> *if Atsuya hadn't eaten all that junk-food....*

Hard growing up under the shadow
of such a famous father—
the house a zoo
with all those visitors.

This afternoon Atsuya's neighborhood association ordered
flowers, rented a tent and chairs. Bought dry ice
to preserve the body.

Harvey pours me a glass of wine—red wine—from the bottle
opened last night with Atsuya.

Just when I was missing him, he'd turn up.

Last night   he dropped in.
Last night   we talked for hours.
Last night   it was like he knew.

Daisies

The kiln's loaded. Tomorrow we fire.
I'm hosing glaze off boards
when our neighbor Kubota stops by
and invites me to his bon voyage party
this afternoon at Harvey and Terumi's.

Sensei gestures GO—
or does he flick a fly off his nose?
Yumiko clips daisies from the garden.

> *Take these to Mrs. Kubota.*
> *You can't go there empty-handed.*

Next door we pick up the car and Mrs. Kubota.
I hand her the daisies.

> *Take these to Terumi.*
> *You can't go there empty-handed.*

Daisies! how lovely! Terumi brings
a white-faceted vase fresh
from the kiln. Yellow disks
and white spikes dip
every which way.

How Are You?

This morning Sensei asks
kibun ga ikaga desu ka?
how are you?

Fine, I mutter,
    head throbbing
    from too much *sake*.

Last night we went to Yukako's
    to celebrate the arrival of their new
    second-hand baby grand.

Potters brought thank-you pots
    to the young pianist and cellist
    who came from Tokyo.

Tekyu fell asleep on Sensei's lap.
    After a few bars of Mozart,
    Sensei nodded off too.

Children who finger scales at home,
    who only hear music on radio and TV,
    heard two musicians play in slippers.

Loading the Bisque Kiln

A bearded and bald Hansel-in-the-oven, Sensei strews rice straw
over the kiln floor. White gloves reach for bonsai planters.
One slips off my board. Shatters.

Yumiko whispers, *when I*
apprenticed, I dropped
a whole board of teapots.

What did you do? I ask.
Sat on the ground and cried.

Last to be loaded are the kids' dinosaurs and snakes.
Sensei seals the doorway.
Slathers mud clay over bricks.

With a flick of a Day-Glow lighter, he ignites
the kindling and a cigarette.

Mantra

Each time

I lift

a board

of pots

I pray to the Buddha

and to every other god I can think of:

SAVE THESE POTS!

Red Wheelbarrow

Sensei intercepts me leaving the house.
Perfect timing! I need your help.

He points to a cornerstone he's about to lay.
I point to the red wheelbarrow.

He points to himself and me.
I point to the red wheelbarrow.

We carry!
I back away.

Carry!
I carry.

Unloading the Bisque Kiln

Annsan, You like saunas?
Sensei's hands swish an hourglass torso.
He steps inside the kiln.

I stack hot pots on boards:
two hundred—less
two I broke,
three he broke.
The kiln's empty.

Yasumi! vacation, Sensei shouts.

The family drives off to Natsumi's school picnic.
The studio is mine!
I switch the radio dial to a Bach partita.

Wedge   Center   Throw.

Annsan! lunch!

Lunch no one is supposed to be home for—
the picnic was only for kids.

After lunch, we dust the ash off pots.
Sensei turns on the radio to a Brahms concerto.
Shoots me a smile. Dials back to Japanese pop.
Shakes my wrist: *BEAT!*
We swat pots with rags tied to sticks.
Ash flies. No one wears a mask.
I don't fetch mine.

Glazing

Sensei swirls glaze onto a giant plate
with a long-handled cup like the ones
used at the temple to cleanse impurities.

I hand him a wet sponge to erase
the errant smudge or stroke.
(Easy for clay to be wiped clean.)

A customer brings Sensei a *kiri* wooden box to sign.
Bowing, the man backs out the door.

Sensei lights a cigarette. *Pressure—*
I smoke too much!
I make a face and thump
my head. He laughs.

Thunder. Tekyu runs in,
straw hat on backwards,
black ribbons tickling his nose.
Hands me my damp socks.
Yumiko follows, arms filled
with rained-on clothes.

Suddenly Tekyu falls on the dirt floor screaming.
Sensei squats beside him. Says in English, *Tekyu on strike.*

Cup Lost in Translation

Sensei: *You don't hold a glazed cup
by the rim!*

_____

    (I didn't say
        you think I did
        but I didn't.)

Sensei: *The glaze flaked off
because **you** touched it!*

_____

    (I didn't say
        your glaze
        was so THICK
        it flaked off by itself.)

Follow the Black Smoke

Plume of smoke. Who's firing? Where?
  Multi-chambered *noborigama*
    most troublesome to fire
        walls   crack   at
          each   firing
            a i r f l o w
          hopeless to
        c o n t r o l
      any change
    in humidity
    s l o w s
    the fire
    but oh
    those
        g
        l
          a
        z
        e
        s

Follow the Black Smoke

Loading the *Noborigama*

Balancing a board of morning cups on my shoulder, I duck
the razor-roof, dodge bricks, beams and the red backpack
Natsumi's always losing, set my board on the ground,
show Sensei where I nicked the glaze off a cup.
Don't worry. I fix.
Natsumi runs up. *I broke two display plates.*
Sensei's head pokes out of the chamber. A forty-watt bulb
hanging from the rafters glints
off his glasses. *How did it happen?*
I sat down on the board and the plates jumped off!
Sensei nods. *So that's how it happened.*
He doesn't say next time be more careful.
He doesn't say that'll teach you.
He doesn't say don't ever do that again.
Halfway up the path, Natsumi stoops,
picks up something red.

Noborigama (Daisei Kiln)

Cloudburst

Thunder cracks.
We cover the glaze
just in time. Rain
pings on waves
of corrugated steel.

Let's go to the soba shop!

Heads dip over bowls
of steaming noodles.
Sensei tenor
Yumiko alto
the children piccolos.

Blisters

More than clay, Koeki
loves the children.
It's hard for him to center,
pull up a wall of clay.

Today he has a cold.
Red-nosed, he sniffles by.
Tekyu tugs at his shirt: *let's play!*
Help me stir ash glaze, I plead.

See these blisters!
I open my palms.
Koeki opens his, redder,
puffier than mine.

Sticks and Stones

After an all-night rain, Yumiko hangs
the first load of laundry on the line.
I ladle ash glaze through an increment of sieves

filtering out sticks and stones.
Full pail empties. Empty pail fills.
Tekyu scoops up some stones

and drops them into the glaze.
His tongue clacks with each plink.
The black water clears.

I lift him up to see the floating clouds.
Baka! baka! baka!—stupid! he shouts.
He checks the sky. The clouds

are back where they belong.
He bites the rim of my pail.
Dame desu! Don't do that! I shriek.

Cheeks smeared with tears
he runs to his mother. Hides
in the folds of her skirt.

What happened? Yumiko asks me.
I look at the sticks and stones enmeshed
in tufts of grass. No one here believes

glaze is toxic. We glaze
where the children play.
I tell her Tekyu was eating glaze.

Next morning I'm mixing ash glaze.
Yumiko hangs laundry on the line. Tekyu
croons *rock-a-bye-baby* to a dead frog.

He runs over and flips it into the glaze.
Sorry about your frog, I say. He nods.
I lift him up. He splashes clouds.

Red? Not Yet

Sensei bows to the fire gods and lights the flame.
Scrimmed by smoke, Emi on her pogo stick
fades and reappears. Minagawa
a professional fierer arrives
tall and thin as a Giacometti.
He chain-saws twelve-foot planks
into four-foot-lengths.
Jabs the flame—left, center, right.
Guides my arm. My aim falls short.
Rain clangs on the kiln tin roof.
Humidity slows the fire.
Watch out! Sensei shouts
and drives off in his white van.
Watch out? what for?
I look around—everything!
Fire snaps. Chambers steam.
Yumiko brings tea and noodles.
Minagawa uncaps a peephole. *Red?*
Orange flames shoot out. *Not yet.*
Asleep, Minagawa's long limbs are splayed
on the ground. With a smoke-soaked blanket, gray
as clay, Sensei covers him; throws me a tarp.
You sleep too. Our rooster crows: *red? not yet.*

Firing the Noborigama

Address Book

An absent-minded hand
    pocketed it
and somehow it slipped
    into the washing machine.
Yumiko fished it out,
    pages congealed—
names and numbers sealed—
    all of Sensei's clientele.
She brought it to the yard to dry.
    Sun and wind
opened pages, tissue thin.
    Bit by bit,
she decoded script
    not unlike the text
of The Dead Sea Scrolls.

Conversation Over Three Centimeters of Sake

Yumiko: *When I first saw you, I was so surprised.*

Ann: *I know…I know…I read it in your face.*

Yumiko: *I expected someone younger.*

Ann: *I must have good karma to have found you.*

Yumiko: *Karma? What's Karma?*

Ann: *More than luck.*

Invitation

Aiko phones. *Eat before you come.*
I have no idea what foreigners eat.

She picks me up at eight.
We drive down Main Street, empty
of tourists. I look through shop windows
at towers of plates daring
the next earthquake to happen.

At Aiko's, a flock of egrets,
beaked heads snapped to wings,
bed down on scraggly pine.
The porch door opens. Hiru bows;
points to Yasuko, face down
on the picnic table.

Wife drunk.
Not sick?
Not sick. Drunk.

Aiko brings an American fan letter for us to translate.
Hiru reads: "your lizard green glaze...."
I giggle. Hiru spits out a mouthful of brandy.

I'm on my second pot of *sake*—or is it the third?
The yellow cat hops on my lap. Purrs.
I feed her my fish croquette.

Hiru pours another round.
He and Yasuko
are on a macrobiotic diet.

We believe all food
is yin or yang—food
harmonizes us to the cosmos.

Yasuko drools and vomits,
says, *I'm hungry* to no one
in particular. Aiko phones
the *ramen* shop and orders noodles.

Queasy from the stench of vomit,
I admire Aiko's jacket.
Like it? It's yours. She spins me
into the blue and orange sleeves.

Hiru removes the black cloth
from the mirror, put there
to shield the eye
from an accidental
glimpse of death.

Aiko's rhinestone barrettes
strobe rainbows
on the tabby's
question-mark tail.

Sealed behind the mirror,
we two are garnished
and duplicated.

The *ramen* man is here
shouldering a board
of steaming noodles.

Caterpillars

I woke to the whir of helicopters spraying
for tent caterpillars. (Yumiko and I
much prefer the caterpillars.)
We went to see Yumiko's American friend.
Drank tea from glossy mugs fired last week.
Unused to Brooklyn Japanese
    I understood next to nothing said.
She brewed a second pot of tea.
Boiling water raised sodden leaves.
I thought of the caterpillars curled
on leaves—falling.

Where did you apprentice?
  Mashiko.
Who with?
  Oh, some potter.
'Mingei'—folkware—is a hard sell.

Hard self is what I heard
splintering the carapace
of language, my sense of her
blurred as the killing air.

To Talk Shows and Pop Tunes

Sensei slices into a vessel, copying a vase
    from the open page of a magazine.
He's commissioned to make Kitaoji Rosanjin
    reproductions for TV.
Yumiko presses clay into a plaster mold, made yesterday. Out pop
    Rosanjin gourds and fish.
Minagawa throws a board of Rosanjin bud-vases, attaches spouts
    to Rosanjin teapots.
Koeki feeds clay into the pugmill, carries Rosanjin gourds, fish,
    bud-vases and teapots to the yard to dry.
Even I throw Rosanjin saucers. Sensei has me measure
    the diameter with a string. Tekyu waltzes in,
yellow bear on his back. Someone's wrapped him in Yumiko's
    orange *obi*—the one embroidered with gold cranes.

Sunday Afternoon at the Buddhist Temple

1
High school girls in navy pleated skirts
and white sailor shirts spot me,
the foreigner. *Hallo. How are you?*
Will you have English Conversation with us?

I am a bee-yu-tee-ful girl, one says.
The others raise their hands
to hide smiling teeth.

You are all beautiful to me, I say.

2
Behind the temple is a grave
skewered with prayer sticks—
a deathday cake
for a life blown out.

I see accessories for the dead:
incense burners, flowers,
oranges, grapefruit.
How much the dead need!

Piled on lanterns are stones
found on the ground,
stone on stone.
Even to the withered flowers I say,

you are beautiful to me.

Prayer Sticks

Rice Paddies

       Water Fields
bordered by footpaths,
seedlings sprout in plastic boxes.
Except for curled tips
they might be blades of grass.

       Wading Cranes
with backward-bending knees
feed on seed-minnow,
alight, take off, claws
orange as persimmons.

       Women Bent
broad straw hats
satellite moons,
mamasan aprons
white as cranes.

Rice Paddies

Reliquary
for Shoji Hamada, 1894-1978

1

Kiln-warm, Hamada's pots amble along the path,
as we might stroll down the Ginza in twos and threes.
Round-rimmed spectacles perched halfway
down his nose, Hamada inspects
this bowl, that pitcher. Picks up a vase
decorated in wax-resist,
his glasses two luminous moons.
I know Hamada from the stories potters tell,
when he begged his dead kiln
to rouse itself for one more firing.
The glazes stunned everyone.

2

Once I got a fortune cookie that said the onion you are eating
is someone else's water lily. Hamada's farmhouse is now
a museum, the field by the Big Gate paved
for tour buses. Shoji doors open
to a black Eames chair, chests and folkware
he collected from all over the world.
On the back wall, I see a black and white Hamada,
photographed at the opening of the kiln.
Expression quizzical. Bald head bent
over pots begging for his approval.

Shoji Hamada

Sa Myo Ji Temple

Zodiac beasts
   lick their lips
   at oranges on the altar.

Tourists in leather shoes
   fling straw sandals
   onto trees.

I look into a room,
   reluctant to admit
   the light
   of a four o'clock sky.

I see a demon, tall
   as two of me,
   eyes rolled back,
   tongue unfurled,
   sword sharp as words.

Sprawled on the floor lie
   a thousand paper cranes
   that failed to heal
   a dying child.

Have I found
   a dumping ground
   for redundant gods
   and demons—
   for hope gone wrong?

Fire in my hand
A cold ball of fire
Fire which has changed its shape
Hidden in the clay

Kanjiro Kawai

Potters

After the War
Takeshi Shiraishi

Before the war
  my father invited a friend
  to set up a kiln
  on our property.

The war
  changed everything.
  My father's factory
  produced military weapons.

After the war
  one of his former employees
  was appointed mayor.
  Suddenly I was free
  to choose what to be.

My father's friend
  taught me to use the wheel.
  He owned a Hamada plate,
  different from any
  I'd ever seen.

Modest Desire
Gen Murata

The war came.

We had four children

and nothing to eat.

I told Shoji Hamada

all I wanted

was to build a kiln

at the foot

of a mountain

and live

a quiet life.

Gen Murata

Ten Years of Teacups
Gen Murata

Hamada said *make the same teacup again and again.*
I didn't think I could. For ten years
I made teacups. Even now
I practice on the cup
to get the clay
used to my hands.
As sketching is for the artist, the cup
is basic to know and to practice.

One day I asked Hamada if I had talent.
I remember him standing there, his arms
folded around my question.
He pointed to an old man, hunched over the wheel,
turning one flawless vase after another.

We cannot match the skill
of this worker's many-many years.
Your pottery is off-balance—too much
of something—too little
of something else. Form
is proportion. Repeat
what you do now.

Technician turning out one perfect
vase after another

They Come to Stay
Michio Goda

First they appear

as visitors

come back

again and again

stay longer

move in and

enter our lives

as friends

Michio Goda

Thumbprint
Toshio Takeda

I had nowhere to go
      so I came to Mashiko.
It doesn't matter if
      I have talent.
If I see the demand for something,
      I make it.
My style doesn't change,
      I only grow older.
See my thumbprint in this clay?
      Who cares whose it is?
If someone in my family gets sick,
      I can't work.
If I didn't use new clay, think of
      the pots I'd lose.

Toshio Takeda

Cup of Tea
Toru Jinnai

I may be one of the few here who love
Mashiko pottery. I came here wondering
what a pottery town would be like.
It never dawned on me I'd be a potter.

So much traffic—not the country village I'd imagined.
Once I climbed the hill I was surrounded by rice paddies.
From Hamada's gate I saw potters working, drinking tea,
and clay drying in the sun. Pots were everywhere: heaped
in yards, in shops, spilling onto the pavement.

I loved the clay's rough texture,
sense of weight,
glazes the color of soil.

My first day in Mashiko I dropped by Shoji Kamoda's.
He offered me the cup of tea that changed my life.

Toru Jinnai with Gerd Knapper

Big Gate
Hiroya Hirosaki

I heard the Big Gate
    belonged to
    Shoji Hamada.

One day I brought him
    some of my work
    to see.

Even though my pots
    reminded him of his,
    he invited me back.

Clay Drying in the Sun

Unchanging
Hiroshi Seto

Coming from Kyoto,
I found Mashiko fresh
and unchanging. I came here
at nineteen. Four years later
I returned to see the same
apprentices at the same
studios, at the same
wheels, sitting on the same
cushions, making the same
pots. Was Mashiko caught
in some sort of time-warp?
For me and for the rest
of the world, the sixties
meant Vietnam,
Cambodia, student riots.
Sometimes I wonder why
I settled here. Kyoto clay
is processed so no seeds sprout.
Mashiko clay grows grass in a week.
Not first, second or third class, but
fourth class, it's so bad. Still,
I like its earthy texture.

Hiroshi Seto

How Things Fit Together
Hiroshi Seto

I think of how geometric planes
    construct volume,
surface planes
    define form.
A lantern is made of bamboo,
    string and paper;
a barrel from wooden planks
    braced by steel bands;
a drum from a hide drawn taut
    over a round frame;
a volleyball is pieces of leather
    patchworked together.
Even clothes
    conform
to the contour
    of the body.

Geometric Planes
(Hiroshi Seto)

Everything Sells
Tsutsukida

My cousin was a collector.
He quizzed me on which kilnsite
each piece came from.

Why not be a potter, he teased.
Hmmm, I thought. Why not?
He sent me to Mashiko to see Seto.

Seto invited me to tea.
Can I make a living here?
I blurted out,

surprising myself
at being so bold. *Of course!*
Here, everything sells.

Bricks

Harvey Young

I worked as a hod-carrier in Colorado. I thought: you guys,
you'll be carrying bricks forever, but me—I'm going to Japan!
I expected to see pagodas and lanterns,
lacquer bridges, people strolling about in kimonos
but instead, everyone wore gray,
lights were either dim or fluorescent
and everywhere were these ugly cinder-block prefabs.
In Mashiko Seto was building a new kiln.
He put me to work carrying bricks and cement.
A cosmic joke: No matter where I go,
there's a brick waiting for me.

Mashiko Real Estate

Drinking wine on Harvey's deck
we watch a tractor drive
through a field of giant tobacco leaves.

The farmer's sons left.
When he dies
developers will seize the land
and subdivide it into plots.

The Youngs built on rented land.
Their landlord can't evict them
or raise the rent unfairly;
the neighbors would disapprove.

Once a house wears out, it's replaced.
I think of the walls and floors piled
in Sensei's shed, waiting to burn.

Lone Wolf
Hidetake Takauchi

The end of the day,
     couldn't leave,
got a room,
     stayed the night,
next day saw more,
     worked night shifts
at the Tokyo Central Post Office.
     Four of us
rented a workshop
     near the station.
Commuted eleven years.
     Learned the kickwheel
at a commercial kiln.
     Museums and books
were my teachers. I take pride
     in being *ippiki okami*—
a lone wolf.

If I Were a Man
Fuku Uno

If I were a man, I wouldn't be a potter.

In the past women couldn't go near
a kiln for fear that menstrual blood
would contaminate the fire.

Of course wives, sisters and daughters
helped husbands, fathers and brothers.

I was Mashiko's first
woman potter—a freak—
the town pariah.

New kilns are easy to fire
but I can count
women potters
on one hand.

Still—if I were a man....

Fuku Uno

Brought up to Believe
Kazuko Satake

I was brought up to believe I could do
anything I wanted, whether or not
it worked. I learned my ABCs
with Nakamura. He turned down
every woman who applied without
her parents' permission:

> (*soot and cinders?*
> *country bumpkin?*
> *my daughter?*)

Two years always needed
in the studio, kitchen and house,
three days-off a month,

> no time
> of my own,
> no life of my own,

afraid of becoming too mannered
working in Nakamura's style,
knowing I could do everything myself,
I built a house, workshop and kiln
(with the backing of my parents).

My first firing took fourteen hours.
The land around my kiln is damp.
I dug a trench.

> Sometimes
> when I'm tired,
> I wish I were a man.

Daughter of a Samurai
Midori Tanaka

My mother and father were Samurai movie actors.
I studied in Kyoto but Kyoto wasn't for me.
I felt smothered by all that tradition!
Even though Mashiko had twenty
good potters to Kyoto's thousand,
I loved Mashiko's earthy glazes;
I loved it that no one here tried
to be important. I rented a studio
with three other women near
the station, and shelves for firing
at a commercial kiln. Every few months,
I loaded up the car and drove to Kyoto
and sold my Mashiko pottery
at the Kyoto Craft Center.

I Borrow Pottery
Etsurou Kotaki

I borrow pottery to live my life.
I've been brought up with it,
live close to it—it's what I do.

As an historian I know
prosperity peaks
and falls.

Mashiko has lost freshness,
turned into *omiyagi yaki*,
souvenir-pottery.

Who knows
what it will be like
in ten years? twenty years?

Etsurou Kotaki

Tradition
Naobumi Kubota

Isolated in Mashiko
we must struggle
to keep up
with the trends.

When an unknown potter
works in a strange new style
he's laughed at—

How dare he imagine
the modern
can compete
with the past?

Naobumi Kubota

Green
Sui Nagakura

I love pale green copper temple roofs,
mossy stones, soft blue mold
on *omochi* rice-cakes.

My green glaze
just happens in a way
I can't predict.

Not knowing makes the green you see.

Sui Nagakura's Studio

Threat of Immortality

We sip green tea from Nagakura's green
glazed cups. I pick up a bowl,
green as the stones I slipped on
on the way to her studio.
She grabs the bowl
and holds it up, as if
it were a temple offering.

Suppose I sold you this bowl today,
and tomorrow I didn't like it—
wish I'd never made it—
wish it didn't exist.
This bowl I hate
might last a thousand years.

Mashiko Colors
Seitojo Tamaki

Coming from snow country,

I'd never seen green

in winter, wheat

so tall and full,

it glistens.

My glaze is green

as Mashiko winter,

yellow as Mashiko wheat.

Patina

Totaro Sakuma

Rooms once dark,
      fill with sunlight.
      Glass replaces
opaque screens.

Once we sat on the floor
      on cushions.
      Now chairs raise
our point of view.

At the wheel,
      I think of the ways
      we see and use pottery.
These cups we drink from

were made by me
      thirty-five years ago.
      My pottery and I
grow old together.

Our touch
      softens the patina,
      makes the glaze
more beautiful.

Silkworm
Naobumi Kubota

Study beauty with a master,
technique with artisans.

Why wait till
you're highly skilled?

What you make
as a student

hardly matters.
Basic technique

is enough. Leave—
find your way.

The silkworm
casts off its skin.

Stone

Tatsuo Shimaoka

Precious stones

are no more

than stone

Skill and fire

transform

dirty clay

to stone

Tatsuo Shimaoka

Sliced Space
Takeshi Shiraishi

A pitcher
is ready
to receive

If I cut
into the center
I cut nothing

I open
my space
to you

Even when
I think
I understand

do I understand?

Clay on the Wheel

One day, a friend asked Shiraishi
how he'd glaze the pot on the wheel.

He only thought of it as it was, a lump of clay.
He shut his eyes until the clay

became the back of a woman—
the most beautiful form in the world.

Seto's Empty Cup

Here's an empty cup on the table.

       (my empty cup)

Our eyes drift toward it as we talk.

       (celadon—palest green)

A minute ago it held tea.

       (I'm still thirsty)

Empty, it's a prop to express the beauty in our lives.

Pine Roots
Totaro Sakuma

The mountains surrounding Mashiko

are planted with red pine.

I like to imagine the pine roots

digging into clay,

clay raising pine trees,

the pine,

clay's gift to fire.

Repetition
Tatsuo Shimaoka

Do you care

if this cup

is exactly like

so many

other cups

that have passed

through centuries?

Repetition

Clay Cloud

Naoyuki Matsubara

Friends I drink tea with

say my pottery

doesn't draw

attention to itself.

People are apt

to pass it by.

I want to make

something

odd and great

like a cloud.

Naoyuki Matsubara

Coffee Ceremony

Yasuda slips a cord beneath a spinning cup,
frees it from the cone of clay. Leans
over the hibachi. Agitates coffee beans
blackening on white-hot coals.
The fragrance masks the scent of clay.
Caught up in the ritual, I see the grinder
whirl faster than the wheel.
Simple gestures. No word spoken.
Nothing to disrupt the shift
between life and art. Yasuda lifts
the iron kettle off the fire,
pours water, on the verge
of boiling, through a store-bought filter.
The coffee steeps—an alchemy of liquid amber.
He hands me a crackled celadon cup. I raise
it to my lips, breathe the elixir of steaming coffee.

Takeshi Yasuda

Edgy

Shoji Kamoda

At first I thought pottery was unclean, unsanitary.
    Have you noticed that musty smell
pottery-lovers have, as if they belong
to an old and decomposing world?

If a man tires of his wife,
    he looks for someone new.
Living in Mashiko, I felt edgy.
I needed a change, so
I moved to Tono.
I'm there six months
and in Mashiko six months.

Mashiko is near Tokyo, where the most sophisticated
    liberal and open-minded people live.
Perhaps there's no place like it.

Shoji Kamoda

Squat Pots

Kamoda sat cross-legged on the deck, stroked a pot,
reached for another, any would do.
        The sun cast shadow-leaves
on Kamoda and his pots.

I saw him twice: two Kamodas:
first time, bearded, hair short; pots striped;
last time, clean-shaven, hair feathering his collar; pots polka-
        dotted.

Once while he was still alive, I dug up a plate
from a discard pile, where potters bury their mistakes.
On the back was Kamoda's seal—

a plain beige dish,
        ash-glazed,
        no stripes,
        no polka dots,
        none of his PIZZAZ,
        unchipped—HIS.

No Good at Words
Shoji Kamoda

When I read a book
I might remember a sentence or two I like
but I can't sum up the plot.

Maybe it's true for all Japanese.
Our culture is legless,
can't convey ideas.

I look at a Dürer—
the meaning is clear.
The Japanese brush plays tricks.

Often when we speak,
our meaning is lost.
We call this

pretending not to know.
We Japanese are silent
even when we speak.

Notes

Names in "Clay," in order of appearance:

Yukako Hayakawa (b. 1948), assisted in the interviews of Mashiko potters, and then moved to Mashiko to become a potter.

Naobumi Kubota (1927-1995), potter neighbor of the Kawajiri's.

Hiroshi Kawajiri, Sensei. the honorific name for teacher and master craftsman.

Yumiko Kawajiri (b. 1848), Sensei's wife and a potter.

Kawajiri Children, Natsumi, eight; Emi, five; and Tekyu, two-and-a-half. (Girl, girl, boy.)

Atsuya Hamada, farmer-son of Shoji Hamada and neighbor of Harvey Young.

Harvey Young (b. 1945), a California potter who apprenticed with Hiroshi Seto, and returned to Mashiko in the early seventies.

Minagawa, firing-technician and potter.

Koeki, weight-lifter and businessman who helped in the studio after work.

Aiko, Hiru and Yasuko are pseudonyms.

Shoji Hamada (1894 – 1978), "National Cultural Treasure" and Master-Potter of Mashiko until his death.

Names in "Potters," in alphabetical order:

Michio Goda (1910 – deceased)
Hiroya Hirosaki (b. 1933)
Toru Jinnai (b. 1943)
Gerd Knapper (photo only)
Etsurou Kotaki (b. 1933)
Naobumi Kubota (1927-1995)
Naoyuki Matsubara (b. 1938)
Gen Murata (1905-1988)
Sui Nagakura (b. 1940)
Totaro Sakuma (1900-1976)
Kazuko Satake

Hiroshi Seto (1941-1995)
Tatsuo Shimaoka (b. 1919)
Takeshi Shiraishi (1934-1999)
Hidetake Takauchi (b. 1937)
Tochio Takeda
Seitojo Tamaki (b. 1948)
Midori Tanaka
____Tsutsukida (b. 1942)
Fuku Uno (b. 1942)
Takeshi Yasuda (b. 1943)

Harvey Young (b. 1945)

Given name precedes surname. Japanese reverse the order. I've
dispensed with the honorific "san" for adults and "chun" for
children.
In "Potters," wherever a potter's name follows the title, the "I"
refers to the potter. In the poems without a name, the "I"
refers to the poet.